Our Global Community

Schools

Lisa Easterling

Heinemann Library
Chicago, Illinois

Customer Service 888-454-2279
Visit our website at www.heinemannraintree.com

Designed by Joanna Hinton-Malivoire
Photo research by Ruth Smith
Printed and bound in the United States of America in Eau Claire, Wisconsin.   021314   008026RP

15 14 13
10 9 8 7 6 5 4 3

The Library of Congress has cataloged the first edition of this book as follows:
Easterling, Lisa.
  Schools / Lisa Easterling.
    p. cm. -- (Our global community)
  Includes bibliographical references and index.
  ISBN-13: 978-1-4034-9400-9 (hc)
  ISBN-13: 978-1-4034-9409-2 (pb)
  1. Schools--Juvenile literature. I. Title.
  LB1513.E17 2007
  371--dc22
                            2006034298

Acknowledgements
The publishers would like to thank the following for permission to reproduce photographs: Alamy Images pp. **4** (Dan Atkin), **10** (Blend Images), **12** (Stock Connection Blue), **13** (Hornbil Images Pvt Ltd), **16** (Royal Geographical Society), **17** (Danita Delimont), **19** (Sue Cunningham Photographic); Corbis pp. **5** (Michael Prince), **6** (Michael Prince), **7**, **8** (Creasource), **11** (Anders Ryman), **14** (Dean Conger), **15** (Tomas Van Houtryve), **18** (Gideon Mendel), **20** (Gideon Mendel), **21** (Karen Kasmauski), **22** (Creasource), **23** (Michael Prince; Creasource); Getty Images p. **9** (Taxi).

Cover photograph reproduced with permission of Alamy/Photo Resource Hawaii. Back cover photograph reproduced with permission of Alamy/Blend Images.

Every effort has been made to contact copyright holders of any material reproduced in this book. Any omissions will be rectified in subsequent printings if notice is given to the publishers.

The paper used to print this books comes from sustainable resources.

Contents

Schools Around the World

Children go to school.

Children learn at school.

Schools have teachers.
Teachers lead the class.

Schools have students.
Students learn together.

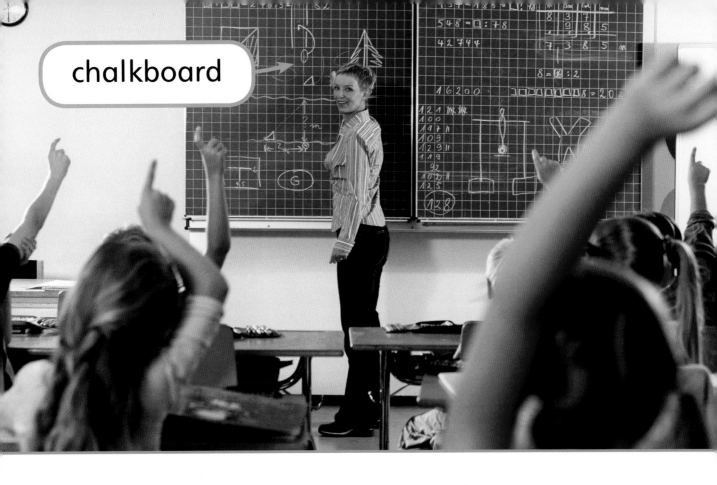

chalkboard

Schools have chalkboards.

Schools have books.

Getting to School

People walk to school.

People ride bikes to school.

People ride buses to school.

People ride boats to school.

Types of Schools

Schools are in big cities.

Schools are in small towns.

Schools are outside.

Schools are in homes.

Some schools are only for girls.

Some schools are only for boys.

Working at School

People work alone at school.

People work together at school.

School Vocabulary

chalkboard

teacher

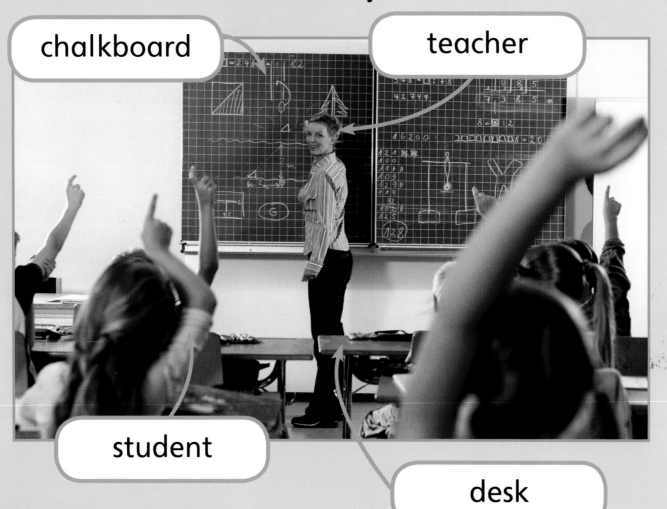

student

desk

Picture Glossary

 **chalkboard**   large board that a teacher writes on

 **teacher**   person who leads a class

Index

Note to Parents and Teachers

This series expands children's horizons beyond their neighborhoods to show that communities around the world share similar features and rituals of daily life. The text has been chosen with the advice of a literacy expert to ensure that beginners can read the books independently or with moderate support. Stunning photographs visually support the text while engaging students with the material.

You can support children's nonfiction literacy skills by helping students use the table of contents, headings, picture glossary, and index.